BEST WISHES!
FROM
Harold & Jo

I am grateful to my son David, my daughter, Liz, and to Titi Tshihiluka for helping me prepare this book and for making a wide variety of often helpful comments.

Above all I thank my daughter Jo for her drawings and that she and her husband Alex Hooper have kept me up to the mark.

The book is written in memory of my wife Erica and our many travels in Greece.

First published 2012

Text Copyright 2012 Harold Mattingly; Drawings Copyright 2012 Joanna Mattingly; Design and Layout Copyright 2012 Pasticcio Ltd. Set in Century Schoolbook 11 on 12.5
Published by Pasticcio Ltd., Bosvathick, Constantine, Falmouth, TR11 5RD
Registered in England No 5125728   01326 340153   www.pasticcio.co.uk

ISBN 978-0-9570311-1-1

Pasticcio

Two coins from Syracuse (c.465 BC)

Coins and Travels in Greece

An introduction to the coins of ancient Greece
with reminiscences of visits by numismatist

Harold Mattingly

Drawings by
Joanna Mattingly

Edited
Stephen Tyrrell

Toddlers chase pigeons
in the main square at
Napflion while we drink
Greek tea, lavender tea
and a Capuccino freddo.

20·5·09

Napflion

An old house seen from the New Acropolis Museum Restaurant

Cretan-type pots
at Apollonian Hotel
Apartments

24 5.09

Contents

A map of the Aegean is on page 10.
A map of the city states is on the rear endpapers.

ATHENS
& GREECE
18 May — 1 June 2010

A Loutroforai fragment
(handle) with dedicatory
inscription

3rd reads ΙΕΡΑΝΥΝ ⊕ ΗΣ

The first pages from two of the sketch and note books of Joanna Mattingly

Preface
Dorothy J. Thompson
Fellow of Girton College, Cambridge

I have known Harold Mattingly for almost half a century. His enthusiasm for, and enjoyment of, research into the coinage of the ancient world has remained constant over the decades. His sometimes controversial views are refreshing – and often ultimately adopted.

It is a delight to find that in his eighty-ninth year he wishes others to share his interest not only in coins but also in the wider history of Classical Greece, combined here with something of the pleasure he has gained from the people, the landscapes and the life of modern Greece. When by chance in 2009 we met up in Attica and then in Laconia (Mystra) in the course of one of his recent travels, so finely illustrated in this study, the depth of his continued interest and enthusiasm were clear to us all.

I hope that many will take the same pleasure as I do in this short introduction to coins in contexts both ancient and modern.

"Every room has a Castle View"

Mystra, capital of Morea,
an outpost in Greece of Byzantium, as seen from the Hotel Byzantion.

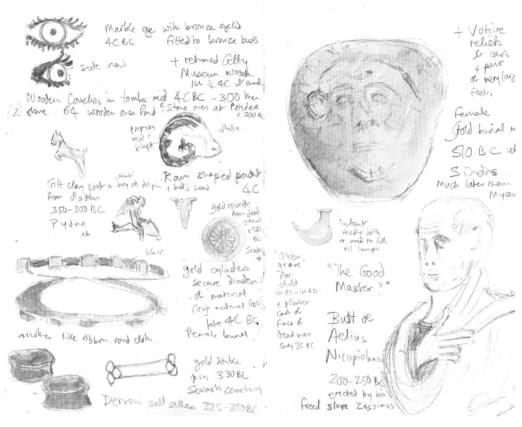

Books filled with drawings and notes

Note: Coin illustrations are not shown at original size and are representations scaled to fit the available space.
The two sides of a coin are distinguished by abbreviations for the words Obverse (the front) and Reverse (the back): (Obv and Rev).

Zeus' Thunderbolt
Elis c.500 BC

Introduction

I have made many journeys to Greece, not just to study the history and coinage, but for pleasure. These visits were often made with my wife Erica, but in later years I have been joined by my family. My older daughter Joanna and her husband Alex have accompanied me on the last two trips and it is from her notebooks, which cover some four hundred pages of drawings and notes, that a selection of watercolour sketches has been made.

These travels around Greece were of course primarily to research ancient sites, to visit museums and to review the early history of Greece and its coinage. We often travelled on local buses and enjoyed trying to ensure we were off the tourist trail. Trips sometimes had a theme, such as that we made in 1976 to follow in the steps of Odysseus, and wherever we went we found friends, renewed friendship, and enjoyed life and company.

We also have the odd memory of animals. One such was Clean, a dirty-coloured sheep dog who waited hopefully at the table when we were staying at Vergina in Macedonia. He was a smaller version of an Old English sheepdog, and rather yellow-white in colour. There were at least two cats, I remember, very curious and hungry and wrapping themselves round my legs. Another night there was a plump and fluffy sheepdog puppy with a penchant for nibbling toes. They were all pets of the neighbours of the hotel and the old black and white sheepdog belonged to the archaeologists who came every summer.

The memories of the people and life are as important as the artefacts, since there is no doubt that the way an older civilisation and social life is brought to life always gave me pleasure.

An orange
juice
freshly
squeezed
at Flo's —
the cafe for
the Greek
National
Gallery

'Where the finest coffee
and people blend.'

21·5·2010

& a carpet of grey-green plastic grass

ΦΥΤΙΛΗΣ

olive oil stain

COMING SOON

Footballs
for sale
in nets.

Paper
Shop!

Ice cream dish

View from Taberna Τάσΐρα
Crowd of men watching football next door
(25·5·2010)

Lamía — cacophony
of buildings in square
but what is Coming Soon?

Street scenes, food and drink

I will always remember when the studio of Pheidias, the great sculptor, had been found at Olympia. The studio site contained pottery datable to the 430s or 420s BC, a period when Pheidias, having created his statue of Athena in the Parthenon, had moved to Olympia from Athens. The studio excavators found traces of his tools and the moulds used for the gold leaf for the flesh parts of his statues. Among the finds from his studio was a mug on which was scratched the words 'Fidio Emi', or 'I belong to Pheidias'. That this mug could be Pheidias' own seems almost too good to be true and brings us in direct contact with the sculptor and his times.

Pheidias' Cup,
showing the inscription
on the base

Many have written of the pleasures of sunshine, wandering unknown mountains and villages, meeting new and friendly people, and considering one of the world's most important and interesting civilisations.

I recall many meals in small tavernas and cafes which have given me more delight than gourmet meals in luxurious surroundings. I have enjoyed bus rides, and the occasional car venture even when we have become irretrievably stuck. For instance, we went off the tourist track to the Bronze Age settlement of Gla, which was once an island in a lake. As the track got rougher and rougher, we ploughed into a deep puddle and got completely stuck. We needed a miracle and within five minutes a miraculous tractor arrived to pull us out. Gla is now known to us as 'Glue'.

Tourists will visit the principal museums, but there are many smaller local museums that are often overlooked but full of items that might, in another country, get top billing.

I hope others will wander there as I have. I also hope, as I write in 2012, that the current financial problems of Greece will result in its becoming the most desirable and inexpensive of places to visit.

Alex's coffee
pot
NATIONAL
MUSEUM
GROUNDS

Towns, cities and countries of the Aegean
Reproduced under free licence

Landscape and Early History

The landscape of Greece goes a long way to explain its history. Much of the area of modern Greece is composed of mountainous terrain. Several Greek cities including Corinth and Athens were dominated by minor mountains like Acrocorinth and the Acropolis. The Greeks regarded the range of Mount Olympus in Macedonia as the home of the Greek gods Zeus and Hera and their numerous offspring.

The mountains could be thought to have provided Greece with defence from invasion particularly as the pass at Thermopylae was much narrower than at present. However, even Thermopylae could be outflanked and famously, in 480 BC, Xerxes and the Persians heard from a traitor of a secret path and were able to attack the Greeks at the side and the rear.

Sparta was long protected by its great mountain ranges on both its east and west sides. Although they failed to take Sparta itself, the Theban army finally broke through the mountain range in the 360s BC and so reduced Sparta to a second rate power.

Mountains divided Greece into separate states, though in time the sea provided easier communications between cities and states and so although it can be said that the mountains divided Greece, the sea could unite them and the sea provided the trade that made the cities of Greece central to the activities of the ancient world and provided the riches that allowed them to develop. The importance of the sea for the Greeks arose not just from trade but because much of the Greek population lived on islands off an extremely long and windy sea coast.

The temple of Poseidon, the god of the sea, at Sounion was the first sight that merchants and others would have in approaching Attica from the sea. It was

Sounion - Temple of Poseidon

The temple of Poseidon at Sounion

said that from this promontory you could see the tip of the spear of the large statue of Athena Promachos (the Champion) on the Acropolis. This statue, like the equally impressive gold and ivory statue of Athena in the Parthenon and that of Zeus at Olympia, were the masterworks of Pheidias the sculptor.

Sounion was part of that silver mining district of Athens, from which came that huge production of silver tetradrachms which funded the Athenian Empire.

Many Greek coinages show sea creatures such as the dolphin and octopus. One dolphin story tells how Arion of Corinth, on a voyage to Sicily, was robbed by pirates and thrown overboard. Saved by a dolphin, he rode it back to Corinth. The coinage of Tarentum, which was part of the western Greek colonial world, has the boy Taras, son of Poseidon riding on a dolphin. Poseidon was not only the god of the sea, but also of earthquakes.

Obv: Dolphin
Rev: Owl
Phoenicia: Tyre
c.460 BC

A Time of Earthquakes

Athens is on the very edge of the earthquake zone. During my visit to the fourth floor of the numismatic museum, the whole building was badly shaken by an earthquake, which seemed to go on and on. The curator was ready to hide under the desk before it stopped. Although this was a relatively minor tremor, it made a great impression on me, yet was nothing compared to the real earthquake damage that we then saw on the Peleponnese.

Erica and I stayed in a hotel at Andhritsena in Arcadia where earthquakes had caused quite a big hole in the wall. We had a fantastic journey to get there from Olympia. Almost all the way the bus driver had to negotiate teams of army volunteers repairing earthquake damage. Whenever the driver passed a shrine, he took his hands off the wheel and crossed himself. We'd rather he had kept his hands on the wheel!

An octopus design
Eretria, Eoboia
c.510 BC

We were lucky to have visited the temple of Apollo at Bassae and seen it in its proper state before it was wrapped up in green cellophane like a big cake. Before modern earthquake damage, the temple was pretty complete apart from its roof. The temple was Doric in date, c.450 BC or a bit later, although the sculptured frieze and some statues had been taken away to the British Museum. I suppose if the Elgin Marbles ever went back to Athens, the Arcadian authority might also want to reclaim their frieze and statues.

Early Greek History

In the Bronze Age (1600-1200 BC) Greece and Crete were dominated by powerful kingdoms with impressive palaces. The earliest of the palaces, built around 2000 BC, were in Crete and the palace at Knossos and the culture of that people is known as Minoan. This title comes from the legendary king Minos whose power was exercised mainly over the seas. An important element of Minoan culture was the snake goddess.

This early Minoan civilization spread to the Greek islands and particularly to the island of Santorini which used to be known as Thera. Here, at Santorini, a Minoan palace civilisation flourished from c.1800-1500 BC. Splendid wall paintings found at Santorini reflect the style of the wall paintings in Knossos, especially one that shows blue and red monkeys. Other frescoes seem to show sea battles. Many of these have however now been removed to Athens with replicas left at Santorini.

Santorini was destroyed by a tremendous earthquake around 1500 BC. Some scholars have connected this destruction with the myth recorded by Plato of a civilisation called Atlantis which disappeared below the sea. Other scholars have related the collapse of the Minoan civilisation in Crete to this catastrophe, although since the Cretan palaces seem to have existed for a further 150 years, this great earthquake may not have been the finishing blow.

About 1400 BC Minoan Crete came under the control of the rulers of Mycenae, Tyrens and Pylos, which were the three most important powers of mainland Greece at this time.

Snakes of the snake goddess
1250-1180 BC
Mycenae Museum

Fira - Museum of Prehistory

The wall-painting of the Blue monkeys Beta 6 room Akrotiri

The wall paintings of the Blue Monkeys from Santorini
Fira: Museum of Prehistory

Mycenae

The late Bronze Age fortress, the Palace of Agamemnon, dominates a fertile plain ringed in with mountains.

Mycenae 'Agamemnon' mask

My first visit to Mycenae started by our watching the bus being loaded with baskets of chickens and yoghurt, a large pane of glass and a birthday cake in cellophane wrappings. We drove until a signpost announced that it was six kilometres to Mycenae, when the driver then left the road to deliver the assortment of packages to the nearby villages. The cake turned out to be for a garage whose proprietor, the birthday boy, ran out to receive it. It was only when deliveries were complete that the bus could resume its journey to Mycenae, fetching up at the restaurant Eleni, named after Helen of Troy. From the restaurant, we were able to pass through the Lion Gate and visit the Palace of Agamemnon.

The story of the war waged by Agamemnon, after the abduction of Helen of Troy by Paris, is recorded by Homer. Troy fell after a long siege at about the same time as Mycenae was destroyed around 1200 BC. Greek traditions for the date of the siege of Troy were about right. The Mycenaean Empire was destroyed in its turn around 1200 BC by invaders who arrived through Thrace from the East.

Boar's tusk helmet with cheek guards Mycenae 14-13thC BC

Heinrich Schliemann, Mycenae's first excavator, thought that one gold mask from the royal tombs was the very mask of Agamemnon although it was in reality the 'portrait' of a king four centuries before Agamemnon.

Bull vase painting (detail). Beaked jug with octopus, Berbati Chamber III 1250-1300 BC
Detail of lyre player from Krater, Naphlion, Evangelista Chamber Tomb IV 1350-1250 BC

Mycenae: The Lion Gate and Citadel

Sources for Greek History

For the Greek Bronze Age we have no contemporary sources. The Homeric poems known as the Iliad and the Odyssey are the earliest sources, but were transcribed some 400 years after the time of which they tell in the 8th century BC. The poems record many memories and tell us of features in Bronze Age life – the palaces, myths of warfare, chariots, shields and helmets, for instance.

The Trojan horse

Evidence from pottery suggests that the poems were widely known in the 7th century BC. The museum at Mykonos has a large pot of about 650 BC which includes a depiction of the Trojan horse with the hidden warriors, although the capture of Troy by a horse full of Greek warriors is a later addition to the story, since the Iliad ends with the war still ongoing. Another pot of this date from Athens shows the story from the Odyssey of Odysseus' dealings with Cyclops.

In 1976, we decided to travel in the steps of Telemachos son of Odysseus. Telemachos, seeking news of his father, went first to Sparta where he was entertained by Menelaus and his wife Helen of Troy. From Sparta he went to Pylos to meet the aged Nestor but saw only his sons. Nestor was the oldest of all the Greeks at Troy and took no part in the fighting but was a valued advisor to Menelaus and Agamemnon. I remember hearing a lecture by Carl Blegen, the excavator of Pylos, who described the extra steps into the bath there as perhaps reflecting the reality of a very old king.

The blinding of Cyclops

From Pylos we went to Ithaca, not knowing then that some modern scholars now deny that modern Ithaca is Homer's Ithaca. Instead they think Homer's Ithaca was a part of Cephalonia which was once separated from the rest of the island by a now disappeared branch of the sea.

The Iliad and Odyssey remain part of modern Greek culture and knowledge. Even in the 1980s ordinary Athenians could quote from these books, as I discovered on the last night of a trip to Athens. That evening two rustic Athenians got the cook's little son to do a dance. When I asked what his name was, he replied 'Leonidas'. So I said 'Oh yes, Thermopylae and the 300'. 'Yes' they said, 'against the Persians and we beat them'. The two countrymen then quoted the first five lines of the Iliad and when I countered with the first five lines of the Odyssey in the original Greek, we became blood brothers.

From 800 BC onwards, during the Greek Dark Age, the principal source is the historian Herodotus, who tells the stories of the Persian wars and gives scattered information on the preceding centuries. He records little about events in Greece after the victory over Persia and Xerxes in 480/479 BC.

For the growth of the Athenian Empire and the Peloponnesian war the one contemporary source is Thucydides. He was much more interested in the political development of Greece and is thought to be generally accurate in his account of the war. As an Athenian general, he failed to save the key Athenian city of Amphibalis, which meant that that town came permanently under Spartan control. Thucydides was exiled for thirty years as a result of this failure.

The harsh landscape of Arcadia, where happiness is associated with shepherds.
In reality, this is a harsh land suitable only for goats.

Thera — The Spring fresco
only in-situ Akrotiri fresco
rocky
local
landscape
+
swallows
See also
'Crocus'
gatherers'
fresco'
same
Painter.

'Bed' found
in this room
when plaster
poured into
space where
bed had been

shelf

Thera: The Spring Fresco, the only Akrotiri fresco found in-situ,
now in the National Archaeological Museum, Athens. 1400 BC

yellow (once black)

red

red

Triple headed sea monster with jutting beards,
or three-bodied demon from porous pediments on the
Acropolis excavated 1886-8 — Doric temple ? Hekatompedon
c 570 BC
reminds me of painting of one of Luttrell's of Dunster Castle, Somerset
about 1,000 years later — depicted with naked torso emerging from sea.

Triple headed sea monster c.570 BC
Acropolis excavations of 1886-8

Coinage

The concept of coinage was a relatively late component in developing civilisations. It may seem surprising that complex societies were quite viable without a coinage. In the Greek Bronze Age, for example, there was no coinage but rather, a complicated control of society and trade based on systems of barter and product control. Similarly, the Persian Empire had no need for coinage except for foreign trade and also operated on systems of barter and product control. Such Greek coinage as came into the later Persian Empire was treated only as bullion and as a result many coins in Persian hoards have gashes made to reveal their metal content or have been quartered into smaller parts.

Persian King
Persia c.485-450 BC

The first currency was made from lumps of metal, which might be of iron or of more precious metals. The development of a coinage meant that a lump of metal, when stamped, was therefore guaranteed by the issuing authority as of a certain weight and purity, meaning that there was then no need to weigh every lump of metal.

In 'striking' or making a coin, a weighed lump of metal was placed between two dies. The lower die was fixed in an anvil and the metal placed over it. The other die was then placed on top of the metal and struck very hard with a hammer. Striking was done either on cold, or, more commonly, on heated metal.

The advent of coinage allowed increasingly sophisticated government and permitted the Greek cities to experiment with all kinds of political systems and governance ranging from tyranny through oligarchy to democracy. Among these alternative political systems in Greece, democracy was in fact rare. Its invention and operation by Athens had little effect elsewhere and then only where there was direct Athenian influence or control.

The issuing of coins started around 560-546 BC with King Croesus of Lydia in west Asia Minor, (who remains famous to this day in the phrase 'Rich as Croesus'), and his Greek neighbours.

The first metal used was electrum, a mixture of gold and silver. Croesus was the first to strike separate gold and silver coins. Greek states only struck silver, except in emergencies, as when in 406 BC Athens struck a short-lived gold coinage. Cyzicus in north Asia Minor continued to use electrum coins with only a stamp on the reverse and these were an important currency in the whole Black Sea area until c.350 BC. Its coin types

Obv: Foreparts of lion
and bull:
Croesus 561-546 BC
Lydia

showed a wide range of deities, such as Nike or Victory.

Although larger coins are sometimes found, the more common and standard Greek coin was a four drachma piece known as a tetradrahm. In Thrace twelve drachma pieces were minted, probably to be exported as bullion or tribute to the Persian Empire, where they are often found. Their designs are mainly agricultural and show oxen and farmers and so on.

In c.465 BC Athens struck some splendid ten drachma pieces celebrating sea and land victories over Persia which took place near Cyprus. Almost at the same time Syracuse struck equally remarkable ten drachma pieces, possibly in rivalry with Athens, but which celebrated victories closer at hand than Persia. The Athenian pieces are very rare and the number of surviving specimens was doubled by the discovery around 1980 in Asia Minor of a hoard which included them.

Obv: Portrait head
Cyzicus
c.350 BC

Obv: Nike
Cyzicus c.500 BC

Obv: Quadriga war chariot with lion below
Rev: Arethusa
Syracuse c.465 BC

Obv: Hermes with
oxen-drawn cart
Thrace-Derrones
c.520-500 BC

 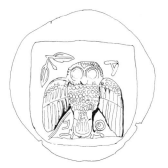

Obv: Athena   Rev: Full frontal owl
Athens c.465 BC

Silver Coins
The Owls, Foals and Turtles

In practice, silver coinage never travelled far from its issuing city, unless it was used for the payment of dues. The exceptions to this generality were the coinage of Athens, Corinth and Aegina, which became so familiar to the trade routes of Ancient Greece that they acquired nicknames: 'owls', 'foals' and 'turtles'.

The Owls of Athens

The first Athenian coins were two drachma pieces with varying types, but around 525 BC these were replaced by tetradrahms with Gorgon obverse and a lion head or bull reverse. Then around c.510 BC tetradrahms bearing the head of Athena and her owl were introduced and became the standard type throughout the coinage, recognized by the nickname owls. A unique tetradrahm with the owl facing left was used to seal some supplies in the Palace of Dareios c.490 BC.

Obv: Athena
Rev: Owl
Athens c.440-430 BC

Rev: Lion's head
Athens c.530-520 BC

Obv: Athena   Rev: Owl
Athens 490 BC

Obv: Female head   Rev: Owl
Lycia-Kharai c.430 BC

The Foals of Corinth

Corinth was famous for its commercial position on an isthmus. Periander, a 6th century BC tyrant, planned a canal through the isthmus but this was long forgotten when a serious start was made on the canal by Nero in AD 67-8, only to be abandoned as too expensive by the Emperor Vespasian after the civil war that followed the fall of Nero. Corinth's coinage standard types were the winged horse Pegasus and the head of Athena, the winged horse giving the coins the nickname foals.

Rev: Athena
Corinth 470-450 BC

Rev: Athena
Corinth 450-440 BC

Obv: Pegasus
Corinth c.550 BC

The Turtles of Aegina

Aegina was, in c.550 BC, the first city to strike coins in Greece. The original design showed a turtle, and it was this that gave the coin its nickname among the Greeks. Around 440 BC the turtle was replaced by the land tortoise but this issue was cut short in 431 BC when the Athenians took over the island. They expelled the Aegonitans at the start of the war with Sparta.

Obv: Turtle
Aegina c.480-457 BC

Tortoise
Aegina c.350 BC

Coin Portraits

Coins are often the only way we have of gaining some idea of the appearance, or even the very existence of some rulers.

The sculptures that you may see in museums and labelled as portraits of Themistocles, Pericles or Socrates were all much later imaginings of their appearance, and not authentic portraits.

Obv: Achaeus
Syria: Kings
220-214 BC

The first portraits found on Greek coins are not of Greeks but of Persians such as Tisaphernes or Pharnabazas, the Persian governors (satraps) who by supporting Sparta destroyed the power of Athens between 412 and 404 BC. These governors proclaimed themselves representatives of the great king of Persia by using the inscription 'BAS' for basileus (king) on the reverse of their coins. After the Persian coins and before the reign of Alexander the Great, portraits are found only on a coin issued by the rulers of Lycia, a state which lay in south western Asia-Minor.

Persian Satraps:
Obv: Tisaphernes   Rev: Owl
c.412-411 BC

Persian Satraps: c.395-394 BC
Obv: Pharnabazus
Rev: Persian king with warship up L.H.side

The first true Greek coin portraits show the successors of Alexander the Great. After his death in 323 BC his descendants divided his empire between them. The centre of the empire, an area equivalent to modern Syria, Lebanon and Iraq, was held by Seleucus. Ptolemy held Egypt and Cyrenie, and Demetrius 'the Besieger' held Macedonia and much of Asia Minor. Cyprus was disputed between Syria and Egypt. From about 300 BC, portraits of kings became more widespread, so providing us with a likeness for many of the later kings of Syria and Egypt.

Philip V of Macedonia
221-179 BC

There are also portraits of Philip V of Macedonia (221-179 BC) and of his son Perseus who lost his kingdom in 168 BC after defeat by Rome.

Perseus
179-168 BC

Obv: Seleucus 1   Rev: Elephant
312-280 BC

Ptolemy 1   Demetrius 1
305-283 BC   162-150 BC

The Eastern Greeks

From the 7th century BC onwards, the Greeks founded colonies on the coast of Asia Minor and on the approaches to the Black Sea. The most important of these were at Ephesus, Miletus, Byzantium and Cyzicus. Byzantium's position on the entrance to the Black Sea established its wealth and importance in Greek trade, especially in the fishing industry. In AD 330 Constantine chose it for his new imperial capital of the East, Constantinople.

The culture of the Eastern Greeks was much influenced by neighbouring kingdoms and especially by Lydia, Assyria, Babylonia and the Persian Empire and this influence marked their art and coins. The coinage of Clazomenai shows a splendid facing Apollo with a swan reverse, and recalls Homer's description of the river Kydnos and of Cleopatra's fabulous barge as described in Shakespeare's Anthony and Cleopatra.

Obv: Apollo
Rev: Swan
Ionia: Clazomenai
c.375 BC

Another Greek colony was Samos, which was a leading sea power in the mid-6th century BC. Under its brilliant tyrant Polycrates, a tunnel was driven through the mountain allowing a water supply to be delivered to the city. You can still walk along the ancient tunnel but there is little headroom and you have to watch your step. The coin types of Samos are the lion's scalp with the cow of the great goddess Hera on the reverse. Hera's temple on Samos was one of the most splendid of its day and its foundations can still be seen today.

Samos was an important ally of Athens after the foundation of the anti-Persian confederacy in 477 BC, but fell foul of Athens and revolted against them in 440 BC. It temporarily secured control of the sea against Athens but was finally beaten and reduced to subject status.

Obv: Lion's scalp
Rev: Forepart of ox
Ionia: Samos
397-396 BC

Cafe of the Greeks, Santorini

The Greek Colonial West

From around 750 BC onwards the Greeks also founded colonies in the foot of Italy and the coastal areas of Sicily. Some of the best preserved Greek temples are found in the Greek West and there are examples at Paestum, Acragas, Selinos and Egesta.

Obv: Apollo
Caulonia,
Southern Italy
c.530 BC

In Italy, a group of colonies centred on Sibaris struck a fascinating series of coins on a common standard. These coins had one side where the type was in relief and with the same type sunk into the coin in the reverse. They were made with two separate dies and it must have taken great skill to properly centre the dies and prevent the coin from splitting. This group of colonies may have been in some form of economic union, and some have suggested that the unusual coinage may have been associated with societies formed from disciples of Pythagoras. Such societies were founded in the mid-6th century BC, although they had been destroyed before the middle of the 5th century.

In the early 5th century BC, several Sicilian cities became rich and powerful under ruling tyrants, men who seized power illegitimately. However, these tyrannies had been abolished by around 460 BC and their departure and fall was, at Syracuse and Leontinoi, celebrated by some splendid coin issues.

Erica Mattingly, the author's wife,
completed a number of architectural ceramic sculptures.
This is a relief sculpture of the portico at Paestum

Trade and Tribute

Coins were used not only for the tribute paid from one state to another but also for trade between states and for payment of mercenary soldiers. In addition, most Greek cities exacted duties on foreign trade, which was central to their state finances.

Greek wine, olive oil and other products were exported over the Mediterranean area. The pottery containers or amphorae in which the products travelled allow us to track this trade, particularly as many of the surviving jars have been found on shipwreck sites. One shipwreck off the coast of Tuscany revealed amphorae, pitch and a bronze ingot stamped with the name caulonia, a city on the toe of Italy famous for its splendid timber for ship building and supply of pitch.

Perhaps the most fascinating of shipwrecks was that found in 1906 at Antikythera, off the north coast of Cyprus. The wreck's hold, from about 100 BC, was filled with rather inferior marble sculptures, but also contained a tangle of metalwork. Once cleaned, repaired and x-rayed, the metalwork turned out to be a kind of clock with aids to navigation and the means of predicting solar and lunar eclipses. There is no description of such a mechanism in ancient writing, although Cicero records that a similar navigational clock was taken to Rome when the Romans conquered Syracuse in 210 BC. The Antikythera clock is now on show in the Athens Archaeological Museum.

Antikythera machine
c.100 BC

Acrocorinth: Old Corinth
& oleander bushes

Amphorae and Pottery

Much of the trade of the east Mediterranean was carried in amphorae. Identification of that trade is helped by the differences in design and shape that existed in different areas. It is relatively straightforward to spot the difference between the wine amphorae of Mende and Chios and the oil jars of Samos.

However, surviving amphorae can also carry other clues. From the scales adhering to the insides of pots from the Carthaginian area, it can be seen that they were used principally for dried or pickled fish, usually tunnies (tuna) or sea bream and were carried between the main centres of the fish trade on the straits of Messina and the entry to the Black Sea at Byzantium.

Cyrene, on the north coast of Libya, was visited by Alexander the Great, who was recognised by the priest of the oracular shrine of Ammon as the son of Zeus Ammon. However Cyrene, a colony of Sparta, was better known for the production of the mysterious plant called silphium, which was a most important trade of the time. This magic plant disappeared after the Classical period and has never been identified. Thought to solve all ills, an ultimate panacea with considerable medicinal qualities, it was widely exported to the Greek world. When Cyrene was taken over by the Romans around 98 BC it paid tribute in silphium. The elder Pliny, who was killed in the eruption of Vesuvius in 79 AD, reported that the treasury at Rome still held at that time a large supply of silphium.

A Chios amphora (top)
An oil jar from Samos

Rev: Zeus Ammon
Obv: Silphium
North Africa
Barce c.380 BC

On Left: The weighing
of silphium for export
(detail of pottery cup)

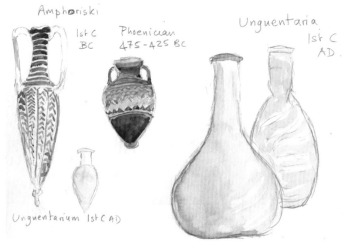

Glass imitating pottery forms in Napflion Archaeological Museum

Pithoi,
Malia, Crete

Big storage vessels (pithoi) continued to be made by local potters for the farmers at Trapsano in Crete until the development of modern containers made this industry uneconomic. These pithoi were in size and technique of manufacture very similar to the storage vessels of Minoan Crete.

However, the ceramic pots required for trade had many other less obvious uses. For example, both pithoi and large amphorae were re-used for infant burials in ancient Greece.

One of the more unusual early uses of pottery was for carding wool. Highly decorated ceramic wool carders were designed to be worn over the thigh and knee and may have been wedding gifts.

Epinetron or Onos, for protection of knee (see below for details)
Piraeus Museum

Attic red-figure *epinetron* by Kleio, painter 440-430 BC, Eretria. Also called an *Onos* and placed on knee for protection from distaff while carding wool. This was probably a wedding present and the decoration shows a women's world scene of wool carding. Another example from c.425 BC has a wedding scene with Harmoneia (Thetis) struggling to free herself from future husband Peleus' erotic embrace.

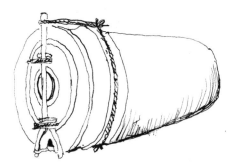

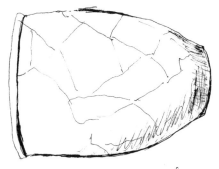

Pottery beehives
A restored hive from Trachones, with
the entrance at bottom

Pottery beehives
Red beehive from the Agora in Athens:
400 BC

Another recent discovery has been the use by the ancient Greeks of pottery beehives. Despite a large number of surviving fragments it was only recently that archaeologists understood that the ribbing inside the jars was the clue to their use, since it was this ribbing that helped the wax to adhere to the inside of the jar. Lots of broken beehives were found in the Mount Hymettos area, famous for that honey which was exported throughout the classical world.

Such pottery hives, which were shown in the paintings on ancient Egyptian tombs, remained in use on some Greek islands and continue to be made to this day.

Two sherds, or pieces of pottery, with fish decoration (top) and a bird.

Interest in these pottery hives resulted in the British Beekeepers' Association giving the British potter Mick Casson a commission to create a pottery hive. We joined him in a visit to the potters at Trapsano in Crete when those works were still active. Mick threw a pot there and my wife Erica, also a potter, helped to fill the kiln. She could always find the right pot for the space, which impressed the potters.

It was at that time we were able to visit a landowner in Attica who not only had a Byzantine church on his estate, but also a collection of huge geometric pots. A notice in Greek had warned us to 'Beware the little puppies' and we were alarmed when the puppies turned out to be huge guard dogs of terrifying demeanour secured on chains.

Water pipes: pointed amphorae from 4th Century AD

Athenian Democracy and Ostraka

In the 5th century BC Athens developed the most democratic society in the ancient world. The running of the city's affairs was in the hands of male citizens and up to five thousand men would regularly meet in assembly to discuss matters referred to them by the Council or the Generals. Voting was done by a show of hands whose numbers were probably then estimated rather than counted, a system that was probably also used for elections.

A panel of six thousand jurors, mainly drawn from the middle class, was used for all kinds of civil and criminal cases. Individual juries could be as large as five hundred in number, making bribery of jurors virtually impossible. Ordinary citizens could stand and win election to lesser offices, since they were chosen by lot.

Athenian democracy involved direct government by the people. It was not government by representatives as is common today. In the 21st century, we only experience 'direct' government through the use of referendums.

However, we should not forget that this was a privileged democracy with an economy which depended on, but ignored the existence of, a body of slaves who, although having some protection from civil law if maltreated by their masters or other citizens, had, of course, no civic rights. Control was restricted to citizens, although some foreigners, long resident in Athens, could enjoy rights or benefits such as owning property or serving in the Athenian army.

The Acropolis & Parthenon, from the Museum

Ostraka

To defend their new democracy the Athenians developed the institution of ostracism. Every year the people of Athens could vote on the behaviour of their political masters. A quorum of 6,000 was needed for the vote to be valid. This voting was done by each voter writing on their broken bit of pottery (the sherd or ostrakon) the names of those they wished to remove from Athens. Anyone unfortunate enough to receive the majority of votes had to leave Athens for ten years, although he retained his citizenship and property and could return and resume his position at the end of the ten years.

Pericles: Ostrakon

Notable 'ostracisms' included that of the great Themistocles, who was the architect of the victory against Persia at Salamis but was ostracised within 8 years of the victory. There was a well organised campaign against Themistocles, which is evidenced by the survival of some 190 sherds written by a limited number of hands.

Another unfortunate was Kimon, a great general of Athens who successfully carried on the war against Persia but was ostracised in 461 BC. His exile and removal from office arose partly from his opposition to new democratic developments and partly from the shift of the Athens alliance from Sparta to Sparta's enemy Argos. However, another factor may have been his personal life since one surviving sherd or ostrakon against Kimon reads 'Kimon get out and take Elpinike with you'. Elpinike was his half sister and their sexual relationship may have been as scandalous as that told around 420 BC in an attack by a comic dramatist.

Ostrakon of Kimon

Another surviving ostrakon dates from soon after the Greek victory at Marathon and shows a Persian archer on the reverse of the sherd. The front reads 'Kallies the Mede', insinuating that Kallies was being accused of treachery with the Medes, a word for Persians.

Despite the virulence of the voting messages, it is a sign of Athenian moderation that we only know of eight people who were certainly ostracised during the seventy years that the system of ostracism worked.

Over time, and despite being a free democracy, Athens developed an empire and control over other Greek cities and peoples, thereby reducing the freedom of those peoples. In turn Athens and its democracy was overthrown by a dictatorship, just as, millennia later, a post second world war democracy was overthrown by 'The Colonels'.

Ostrakon of 'Kallies the Mede'

The Colonels' Motor Cavalcade

The period of 'The Colonels' was one when, as with visits to South Africa during the Apartheid boycott, it seemed inappropriate to many people to visit Greece. Seven years was a long time to stay away. I wanted to go and see what was going on and during my visit in 1969 got caught up with a motorcade. The policemen were going bananas trying to get the traffic out of the way. First came the outriders and two or three big cars, the presidential car, then more despatch riders – all passed so quickly. This probably happened every day during the time of the Colonels.

During this visit I met interesting people at the British School of Archaeology at Athens. It was with some of them that I went to Napflion and also made a further visit to Mycenae.

Oleanders ?

1 June 2010

Women in Antiquity

It is difficult to find out much about the women of the Bronze Age, since we know only of royal women, although they seem to have had more freedom than later generations. Homer seems to give women a more important role. For example, Nausikaa, the daughter of King Alchinuos whose mother was Queen Arete, was clearly the power behind the throne.

Women had few rights in the city states of ancient Greece. They could not usually vote or hold any office, although they could and did exercise power through behind-the-scenes influence on their husbands. Aspasia, the mistress of the Athenian statesman Pericles, was a considerable force in Athenian politics and life.

Later, there were powerful queens among the Ptolemys who came after Alexander the Great, among whom the most famous was Cleopatra. Queen in her own right, she was the last of the line since she was defeated by the Romans, as described in both Plutarch and in Shakespeare's Anthony and Cleopatra. Despite the romantic stories and the traditions of her beauty, her coins show her as middle aged, of no great beauty, but a woman of character.

Bride with
bridal crown & veil
435-420 BC
Acropolis Museum

Cleopatra
c.35 BC

Fresco detail of lower frieze by the altar
Mycenae period

Among the city states, Spartan women were better off than most Greek women. Highly honoured as the mothers of the Spartan warriors, they exercised with the men, had a more important role in religion and festivals and in general were better educated than women elsewhere. Aristophanes' play 'Lysistrata' tells of the delightful Spartan Lampito, who becomes Lysistrata's main ally in the sexual strike by the women of Greece against war. She is sparky, confident and fun. In another play by Aristophanes the women 'in assembly' seize control of the government and begin issuing laws in their own favour. Although this revolutionary idea may have owed something to the teaching of Plato, it is really a piece of comic fantasy.

Women were also celebrated by some festivals at Athens, particularly those for the cult of Artemis in which the women who served her were called 'little bears'.

A small pottery bear, the sacred animal of the goddess Artemis. 4th Century BC.

Temple of Asclepios
Lions help to drain the roof

c. 370 BC
Doric style

19.5.09

Lions at the Temple of Asclepios, c.370 BC Museum at Epidavros

Slavery

Greek civilisations used two forms of 'un-freedom', the first being a land-based serfdom as operated in Thessaly and Sparta and the second being a form of chattel slavery.

Serfdom was forced on the population of Messenia when it was conquered by the Spartans early in the Dark Age. The Spartans tied the Messenians to the land, where they worked their masters' farms and were not allowed to run their own lives. It was not until they were freed by the Theban general Epaminondos in the 360s BC that this changed and they established their own free country, Messenia.

Chattel slaves could be freely bought and sold and the market for slaves was often supported by the actions of pirates and bandits. These slaves came from Thrace, Asia Minor, Syria, Egypt and Africa and if they had any special talents or training reached high prices and were more reasonably treated. Slaves could be freed by their masters after long and good service, but usually had to contribute some money in compensation for the loss of their service.

Slaves formed a considerable portion of the agricultural labour in Attica and in towns were employed in a number of domestic duties and in factories large or small. Some ten thousand slaves were also employed in the silver mines in Attica where conditions were terrible. Often owned by rich men, the slaves were hired out to the mine owners who gained their fortunes in this way.

Such slaves became important to the economic viability of the state. So when, in the last ten years of the war with Sparta, Sparta established a military post in Attica to which thousands of these slaves escaped, it dealt a serious economic blow to Athens.

Treatment of slaves in Athens was fairer than in most other Greek states. They had some protection in law against violent mistreatment and they were valued because of their economic usefulness in a city dependent on trade and manufacture. When slaves were freed they could set up their own businesses and in the 4th century BC one ex-slave called Pasion was able to set up a banking concern.

During the period of Roman supremacy, the island of Delos became a centre for the slave trade and it was said of Delos that as many as five thousand slaves might be dealt with in a day.

The City States of Greece

Traditionally, Greece was a land of individual city states, with different systems of rule and very different traditions. The two states now best remembered were Athens and Sparta, which were often the pre-eminent cities over centuries of competition. However, the many other city states, all of which produced their own coinage, should not be overlooked.

The Athenian Empire in the 5th century BC

After 478 BC, the Athenians developed the 'Free Greek League' against Persia. This league developed to become an empire which extended as far east as Aspendos in south-eastern Turkey. Athens controlled most of the islands of the Aegean but Crete and Cyprus always remained outside their reach. Athens' power rested on its prestige, its navy and its possession of rich silver mines, a situation bettered when, in 437 BC, they secured Amphipolis with control of the gold and silver mines of Mount Pangais. However, Amphipolis was taken from Athens by Brasidas in 423 BC and never recovered. Although they continued to attempt to recover the territory during the 4th century BC, Athens was defeated by Philip II of Macedon.

Athens became increasingly dictatorial in the 5th century BC and a notable feature was the banning by Athens of the coinage of her allies. This ban, known as 'the Standards Decree', was enforced for a time from 425 BC. It also imposed Athenian weights and measures on the allies. Such Athenian interference caused increasing discontent and this contributed to the revolts which were in turn exploited by Athens' enemies, first Sparta and then Persia.

The Athenian Empire was eventually overtaken by its enemies and fell as Persia re-emerged as a power in 404 BC.

Obv: Athena
Rev: Owl
Athens c.440-430 BC

Obv: Europa in tree
Crete: Gortyna
c.325 BC

Rev: Hermes
Crete: Sybrita
c.330 BC

To Left:
Dionysus on ass
Challidice-Mende
c.425 BC
A banned coin

Other coinage flourished outside the Athenian Empire. The fascinating coinage of Crete includes examples such as Europa sitting in a tree or Hermes fastening his bootlaces.

The island of Melos was a colony of Sparta, which refused to join the Athenian Empire. Athens attacked it without success in 427 BC, and required a tribute which Melos refused to pay. In defiance of Athens' ban on silver coinage in 425 BC, Melos continued to strike its own coinage. Examples of these late coins almost all come from a hoard buried on Melos when the Athenians conquered the island in 416 BC. The word Melos means pomegranate and some of the coins therefore illustrate the pomegranate.

Much of the history of ancient Athens is shown in the splendid new Acropolis Museum in Athens. This museum has the friezes and metopes that Elgin, the 18th century collector, didn't take to England. The museum still keeps a large space reserved for those Elgin Marbles which Elgin did remove. Is it not time for Britain to make the friendly gesture?

In addition to a fantastic view of the Acropolis, the museum contains amazing treasures from the Bronze Age onwards. It is also an archaeological site, since underneath the museum are the ruins of shops, houses and baths of the Classical period, which are visible through viewing panels in the floor. Among the exhibits of sculpture dedicated on the Acropolis, are the famous Kouroi and Korai (youths and maidens) of the period before the Persian sack in 480 BC. From the Classical era one of the loveliest displays is of the Nikes (Victories) which once stood on the balustrade of the temple of Victory and date from around 420 BC. One of the Nikes is shown fastening her sandal.

Other exhibits include finds from Mycenae, Tiryns and Santorini. One of the most exciting displays is that showing the Antikythera navigational clock which stands in a gallery of its own.

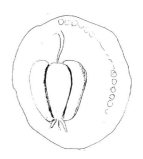

Obv: Pomegranate
Rev: Male head
Melos   c.420-416 BC

Nike (Victory), adjusting sandal. Parapet frieze of Temple of Athena, Athens c.421-413 BC

The Acropolis- 40 years of 'restoration'

Cafe ΕΞΕΔΡΑ
Leonídhio

Where solar panels,
and red chimneys
vie with the
amber cliffs.
Mountainous route
ahead...

20·5·'09

Cafe Efeapa Leonidhio
Where solar panels and red chimneys vie with amber cliffs;
Mountainous route ahead to Sparta.

Sparta

Sparta is set on a big river, the Eurotas, in a lovely setting surrounded by a rich valley and the Taygetus range of mountains. The Spartan people had a reputation for being anti-intellectual and militaristic. It was because they had the Helots, a conquered neighbouring people, to work their lands that the Spartans could concentrate on military prowess.

Although Sparta was sometimes the enemy of Athens, the Athenians retained a secret respect for Sparta and were more usually allies. Helen of Troy (famous from Homer's Iliad) and her two brothers Castor and Pollux, who are sometimes represented on coins by depictions of two amphorae, were prominent in Spartan religion and myth. Spartans are still remembered to this day by their reputation for selfless efficiency in war and hard spartan training in an uncultured state. However, Aristophanes' play about the sexual struggle by the Greek women against war has a sparky, confident and fun Spartan lass, which suggests that perhaps Spartans weren't all that bad.

Sparta was long protected by its great mountains from invasion. The narrow pass at Thermopylae which the Spartan King Leonidas and the 300 defended is now a wide plain. There is a modern, moving memorial to the fallen with an elaborate inscription describing the achievement. On one side, the monument has a reclining naked male figure labelled 'Eurotas' and on the other side a similar female figure inscribed 'Taygetus', symbolising first the wide river and second, the snow covered mountain range.

Obv: Nabis
Rev: Heracles
Lacedaemon, Nabis
Sparta
c.207-192 BC

The mountains also helped hold off a Theban army, although Thebes eventually broke through in the 360s BC to liberate Messinia. Although Sparta itself was not taken, it was from then on reduced to being a second rate power.

For a long time, the city state of Sparta rejected the concept of coinage and continued to use weighed iron as a kind of currency. Eventually the kings and generals of Sparta gave in to the temptations of a gold and silver currency. One Spartan military official was famously accused of keeping 'little owls' in the rafters of his house, the phrase 'little owls' being an allusion to a stash of Athenian coinage.

In later times Sparta occasionally minted coins. Notable among these are the coins of the tyrant Nabis which bear his portrait and, on the reverse, a powerful Heracles. Nabis made the mistake of crossing swords with the Romans which resulted in his defeat and deposition by Flamininus. Flamininus has his portrait depicted on a very rare gold coin which bears his name in Latin.

Flamininus
228-174 BC

Rev: Nike
Gold Coin: Flamininus
228-174 BC

Sparta from the Menelaion Sanctuary.

Best
Dolmiades
in Thebes at
Dionysos
'God of
Wine'
24·5·2010

Dionysus bar, Thebes

restored

dark
ochre
orange

Sphinx

restored

restored

A Sphinx at Delphi

Thebes and the Cult of Dionysus

In the Bronze Age Thebes was the centre of a splendid kingdom. Although few archaeological sites of that kingdom survive, there are many surviving 'tablets' (the administrative documents of the state) and some wonderful sarcophagi with Minoan scenes of bull leaping.

Obv: Lion attacks bull
Challidice-Acantus
c.424-400 BC

Then, for a brief time in the 4th century BC, Thebes was the main military and political power in Greece. In 371 BC Thebes had defeated 'invincible' Sparta, but was, in 336 BC, in turn defeated and destroyed by Philip II, the father of Alexander the Great.

Athenians rather unfairly regarded Thebans and their fellow Boetians as backward and stupid, although the city produced the poet Pindar and the intelligent politician and general Epamondas.

A notable reminder of Classical Thebes is the Taverna Dionysus, named after Dionysus, also known as Bacchus, who was the great God of Thebes. The cult of Bacchus was imported from Thrace, which was culturally backward in relation to mainland Greece. This cult allowed primitive religious orgies to be held for female followers of Dionysus, at which men were not welcome, although the Greek city states eventually succeeded in taming and controlling what they considered a wild country cult.

Dionysus on ass
Mende c.425 BC

These barbarous Thracians had their tribal coinages which include scenes of violent rape of nymphs by satyrs (satyrs being connected with the god Dionysus). Another coin shows a satyr, half man half goat, who carries off a protesting woman as she signals for help with two fingers. Later coins from Thasos have more sophisticated images which even develop an apparent tenderness. The same rape scene becomes transformed into a charming love scene as the woman is no longer protesting, but puts her arm lovingly around the satyr's neck.

Obv: Satyr carries nymph
Thracian Chersonese
c.520 BC

Obv: Satyr and nymph
Thasos c.465-450 BC

Obv: Satyr and nymph
Thasos c.420-410 BC

The coins that bear the satyrs are examples of the many strange animals, birds, demons and monsters to be found on coins, since Greek art and mythology were strongly influenced by the cultures from further east. Mythical animals on coins included sphinxes, gorgons and centaurs. The gorgon was depicted either at full length or as a big grinning head with snakes in its locks of hair. Centaurs are a mixture of the horse and human form. Sphinxes and other monsters were popular not just on coins but particularly so on early Corinthian pottery. The Minotaur, who was part bull, is shown on a Cretan coin and another Cretan coin shows the famous labyrinth in which he was confined.

Obv: Gorgon
Athens c.530-520 BC

EDESSA – Once thought to be Macedonian centre – then Vergina was discovered

Ιεροc Ναοc
Ανα ΛΗVεwc

Candles relecling in water outside chapel

Waterfall at town end

Owls, foals, tortoises and octopuses are nicknames for coins of Athens, Corinth (pega Aegina (with turtles) & Eretria in Nubia   28·5·2010

Another watery place Nymphaeion at Mieza. 3 rock cut cool caves in all Did Aristotle teach here? "Humph" says Harold

Old house Veroia

Details from Edessa, Macedonia

Macedonia

In the 1980s the royal tombs of the Macedonian kings were discovered at the village of Vergina, which was thus identified as Aigai, the capital of the kingdom. All the tombs had been robbed out save one, which contained a gold chest with the bones of the king, his helmet, shield, weapons and many gold and silver ornaments. The tomb also held the remains of the couch on which his body was cremated. This splendid tomb was thought to be that of Philip II, although some scholars remain unconvinced of this.

After the amazing discovery of the supposed tomb of Philip II, a number of other tombs were found. The best of these belonged to members of the royal house, but the others probably represented those powerful Macedonian families who in the 5th century BC had threatened the rule of the main dynasty. These family tombs, like the royal tombs, were decorated with wall paintings. In the remains of an unknown Greek town, now called Mieza, were found other non-royal tombs.

A reclining
Pluto & Persephone
Macedonian tomb: Mieza

A death couch and other items from Macedonian tombs, now at Vergina

Enemies of Philip II tended to regard the Macedonian people as barbarians, despite the fact that after the war against Xerxes, Alexander I had been admitted to the Olympic Games with the support of Athens, implying that the royal house of Macedon was regarded as Greek. Philip II, a distant descendant of Alexander I, issued splendid tetradrahms that showed Zeus and Philip's winning horse and jockey from the Olympic Games.

Alexander
as Heracles
Alexander the Great
363-323 BC

Philip II's more famous son Alexander the Great produced silver coinage showing Heracles, the ancestor of the Macedonian royal kings, wearing his lion skin. The reverse of the coin shows Zeus enthroned with his eagle.

Following Alexander the Great's victory over Persia, Greek culture, influence and coins spread as far as Afghanistan and India.

Rev: Zeus
Alexander the Great
363-323 BC

After Alexander's death in 323 BC, the empire was divided among his generals. Seleucus took Syria and the central provinces of the Persian Empire, Ptolemy took Egypt, Cyrene and Cyprus, and Demetrius 'the Besieger' took Macedonia and much of Asia Minor. The army of the Seleucids in Syria included a formidable division of Indian elephants which are depicted on their coinage.

Obv: Mounted Horseman
Alexander 1
c.475-454 BC

Obv: Zeus
Philip II c.359-336 BC

Macedonian kings:
Rev: Victorious jockey

Obv: Antiochus III

Rev: Elephant
Syria   223-187 BC

DION - The Store

glass
blue eyed
mouse from
bottle base?

Ibis
(enlarged)

gold
earring

- light
green
- litle
ruby
- pearl
(one of pair?)

Recent finds

- dark

Gordian I

Corkscrew
principle
? medical

Dion - bronze coin
Γορδιανός Γ';
(238 - 244 p·x)

OE
oot
Δio

Silver
American
Coin

ΤΥΜΒΟΣ ΝΕΑΣ
ΕΩΕΣΟΥ 2000
3 ἄθημένα αττικά
νομίσματα

Items at Dion, the Macedonian Mount Olympus

Olympia and the Olympic Games

There were four principal games in Greece. These were the Pythian Games, (named after the priestess of Delphi), the Isthmian games at Corinth, the Nemean games near Argos and of course the Olympian Games. From 766 BC, the Olympic Games were held at Olympia every four years. This regularity provides a good basis for much of the chronology for Greek history.

Rev: Running male
Peparethos
c.500-480 BC

The games at Olympia were perhaps the most prestigious in the Greek world and victors were honoured in their own country. It is recorded that in some city states, the city wall was demolished to allow the victorious chariot to enter. The prestige of the games was such that the Emperor Nero, in AD 68, demanded that he should be allowed to compete in all the great games and that they should all be held in the same year. He was of course victorious.

Rev: Nike
Elis
c.450-430 BC

The city of Elis controlled the international festival of Olympia. Its coins show Zeus and Hera, many variations on the theme of the eagle and the thunderbolt of Zeus, and the figure of Victory or Nike. A coin from Pamphylia illustrates the contests by showing wrestlers, with Zeus on the other side.

Rev: Thunderbolt
Elis
c.420-410 BC

Obv: Wrestlers
Pamphylia-Aspendus
c.375 BC

Obv: Hera (?)
Thessaly-Gomphi
c.350-340 BC

The Stadium athletes had to be fit to get here - let alone to run!

Poppies now where Nero raced his chariot at the Phythian games & maybe sang a little = or 21C AD American woman in 20s: wheezing way to top "Is this the last thing

The stadium at Delphi

Theatre

Greek theatre productions were performed by actors who wore masks and who were all men, no matter the sex of the character. Such performances were an important part of city life, and many cities had centres for performances of Greek tragedy and comedy. One of the most famous theatres was at Epidavros, which had room for about 20,000 spectators. Most plots were based on the stories of Greek mythology and in particular the exploits of Homeric heroes. It was exceptional that only eight years after the events it depicted, Aeschylus wrote a play called 'The Persians' about the Greek victories on the sea at Salamis and on land at Platea in 480-79 BC.

Athens was the most important theatrical centre and the playwrights competed there for the prizes of tragedy and comedy in the months of February and March (the two festivals of Dionysus) each year. Plays by Athenian poets such as Aeschylus, Sophocles, Euripides and Aristophanes have survived and are still performed today.

The death of Agamemnon

Productions of Greek tragedy and comedy are still a regular feature of modern theatrical life. At Cambridge, England, a Greek play, usually a tragedy, is presented every three years, in the original language. In 1952, now almost sixty years ago, the Greek play chosen was Agamemnon, a fairly straightforward production which got a terrible review. Cassandra, who is meant to wear the fillets of the priestess of Apollo, looked instead as though she'd got a string of sausages round her neck. Cassandra resisted Apollo's advances and to punish her he gave her the gift of prophecy with the penalty that she would not be believed. The dominant figure in the play is Clytemnestra, who kills her husband Agamemnon soon after he comes back to the palace from the Trojan Wars. When he is trapped in a great robe like a net she stabs him with a sword. Aigisthos, her lover, tries to claim credit for the murder. The chorus charge him with cowardice for leaving the woman to do the job. Early Greek drama influenced and was recorded in other arts. For instance, a remarkable vase painting seems to show the scene of Agamemnon's death, though not the part played in that death by his wife. The other side of the vase shows the revenge for this: the murder by Orestes of Clytemnestra and her lover. Perhaps this vase was painted by an artist impressed by seeing the play.

Obv: Apollo
Amphipolis, Thasos
c.390-357 BC

I once took part in a performance of Aristophanes' 'The Birds'. The matinees were full of school parties of children and teachers who spent the time 'shushing' their pupils, and it was only in the evening performances that the audience was on our side from the start. Nowadays they have sur-titles and translations set over the performance which make it a lot easier to follow.

My wife Erica and I went to the theatre in Thasos for an Aristophanes play performed in demotic Greek. Men, women and children came up from the village, making for a great atmosphere. Behind us were sitting a father and uncle whose two boys sat next to us. The boys didn't know if they could laugh at the naughty bits and were relieved when they saw us laughing and, with their father and uncle, joined in.

Among memories of many theatre visits, that made to Epidavros, the largest surviving theatre, stands out. We went to see a performance of the two Oedipus plays. This had an international cast, but because the face masks hid the actors, it was not until Antigone removed her mask at the end that she was seen to be West Indian.

The production became controversial and had several problems. First, although the theatre is built entirely of stone, the Greek fire service complained that the flaming braziers were a danger. The stage manager was arrested and the actor playing Oedipus fell off the platform and broke his arm. Nevertheless, despite the difficulties, and although the enormous theatre was only about half full, the evening was a success. The moon rose over 10,000 people sitting on the stone seats in the most impressive of performances.

The Theatre at Epidavros

The Cult of Asclepios

The god Asclepios, son of Apollo, was a great healer. His staff of office, wound round with snakes, has become the symbol of the modern medical profession. Because of his reputation for healing, people wishing to be cured by Asclepios flocked to his temples. There they would be welcomed by a priest and settled in cells to sleep over night, since it was believed that in their dreams the god would tell them how they could be cured. As a result communities of doctors grew up around the temples to Asclepios in places like the island of Kos and Epidavros. There were sometimes tame snakes in the temples, since snakes were sacred to Asclepios. Grateful patients dedicated stone, clay or bronze models of their affected limbs or organ in the god's temple. This tradition continues today with similar dedications in Catholic churches around the Mediterranean.

Aristophanes wrote a comedy called 'Ploutos', (which means wealth), which was about two Athenians who take the blind god Ploutos to Epidavros to be cured. They hope that when he has his sight he will distribute wealth to the deserving. Being a comedy it doesn't work out quite that way.

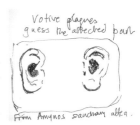

A votive plaque showing ears. Amynos Sanctuary, Crete

Delphi and Oracles

Isolated in a mountainous part of central Greece, Delphi was perhaps the most famous oracle in the Greek world. Individuals and cities would come to consult the oracle about matters of policy or private life. Answers to questions were given by the Delphic priestess called Pythia who would go into a trance and utter ecstatic replies. These replies were then interpreted by the priests, speaking in hexameter verse, in an almost equally mysterious fashion. However, you had to be careful in understanding the oracle's advice. King Croesus of Lydia asked whether he should do battle with the Medes. He was told that if he did so he would destroy a mighty kingdom. Sadly, the kingdom which was destroyed turned out to be his own.

Some cities such as Athens enjoyed a special relationship with the oracle. They paid less for the answers and were sometimes luckier than other cities in the replies that they got. Every four years the Pythian Games were held at Delphi and great crowds would attend.

Delphi profited greatly from victories in Greek wars. Athens, after its victory over the Persians at Marathon in 490 BC, sent splendid offerings to the shrine. The remarkable silver coinage of Delphi was probably made

Obv: Two rams' heads Delphi c.480 BC

Rev: Four sunk squares enclosing dolphins Phocis-Delphi c.480 BC

Delphi - a stunning view which everyone wanted to photograph

possible by these gifts. When the army of King Xerxes invaded Greece in 480 BC he sent one division of his army to raid Delphi. The people of Delphi claimed that the Persian army was driven off by the gods by means of avalanches and storms. But as the Delphic coins are found only in the Persian Empire and not in Greece it seems possible that they represent bribery by the Delphians to persuade the Persians to withdraw. Delphi was accused by the other Greeks of disloyalty to the Greek cause and these coins may reveal part of the reality.

In northern Greece at Dodona near Joannina is the oracle of Zeus. Here, there was once a theatre and temple. The oracle issued some of its answers on oak leaves as well as on stone. It was probably the most important oracle after Delphi. Although the answers written on oak leaves have not survived, some of the answers inscribed on stone to the questions asked of the oracle, can still be seen in the museum there.

Visiting Delphi requires fitness and the ability to climb hundreds of steps. For one visitor the journey did not seem worthwhile. 'Is this the last?' asked the thirty-something American lady, as she puffed her way uphill to the stadium.

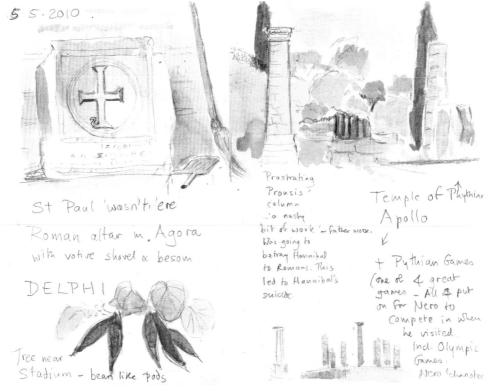

Sketches from Delphi

Black e rans

Lot of
"goat meat
on road to
Monastery
of Timios

Goats on the road to the Monastery of Timios Prodomos

Monasteries and Churches

Travellers to Greece may concentrate on the sites of Ancient Greece, but there have been two thousand years of occupation and civilisation since those days. These include the monasteries and churches of the last thousand years. The remote monasteries in the mountains and the ancient churches are often spectacular and should form an important part of any tour of Greece.

Monastery of St Barbara
closed Wednesdays

Monastery of St. Barbara, Meteora

Meteora

Monastery of St Nicholas Anapafsas
- too much of a climb for Harold

Meteora: The Monastery of St Nicholas

Meteora

Perhaps the most impressive and surprising monasteries are those at Meteora in Thessaly. Dating from the mid-14th century AD onwards, they were built on a series of dramatically shaped rocky outcrops.

Unlike the monasteries of Mount Athos where only men are allowed, both sexes can visit Meteora, although they must be 'decently' dressed. To meet these standards, Erica used her time in the taxi to change from trousers into a dress, which amazed the taxi driver. However, as we were then hauled up to the monastery in a basket at the end of a rope, a strong wind blew the dress around her waist in an entirely 'indecent' fashion.

Today there are two convents among the six surviving monasteries at Meteora. Originally all supplies and humans had to be drawn up in baskets but now suitable rock cut steps lead the tourists to the entrance. Since lunchtime was kick-out time, we'd barely got started when the younger nun who Jo was trying to draw, shut her book with a sigh and went to toll the bell. So we returned in the late afternoon to receive a smile of recognition from the older nun.

Dafni

Another well-known site is Dafni which has fine c.1100 AD mosaics. It occupies the site of an earlier sanctuary of Apollo Daphnaios, from which it has inherited its name.

Dafni

Mystra

Mystra near Sparta is a ruined Byzantine town that flourished from the mid-1200s to 1460 AD. Within its walls the visitor can find over thirty chapels, churches and monasteries, many with mosaics or frescoes in good condition. There is also the palace of the despot, the ruler of the town. This is another site where the climb did not seem worthwhile to another visitor, a German lady who exclaimed:

'You can't go in there. It's all steps'. It was, but we managed.

and all those steps Harold!

Marmara-Turkish fountain at Mystra lower town

Saint Sophia – monastery at Mystra

Frescoes c.1350 survived under Turkish whitewash when it became a mosque for a bit

Side chapel with complete sequence of Life of Virgin Mary – facial detail gone

The life of the Virgin Mary, frescoes c.1350 AD
Side chapel of Monastery of Saint Sophia, Mystra

Hosios Loukas

Between Athens and Delphi is the Monastery of Hosios Loukas, where some monks are still in occupation. Its two churches of 10th and 11th century date are known for their alabaster windows, frescoes and mosaics.

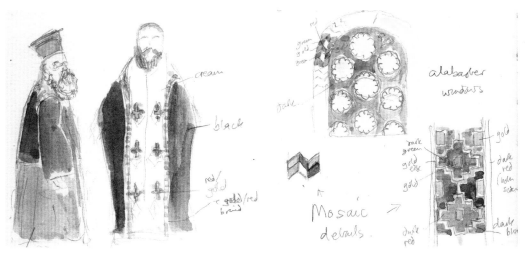

Young monks
with long black hair in pony tails

Interior Details
Hosios Loukas

Hosios Loukas

Churches

Byzantine churches have survived all over Greece. Fragments of ancient inscriptions and sculpture have often been incorporated in the building so they are like mini museums.

One of the best collections of early Christian architectural fragments can be seen in the Byzantine Museum at Thessaloniki and at the church in the shadow of the great Metropolitan church in Athens.

Monastery of Timios Prodomos, near Vergina

Child's painted tomb;
with dog and lace up boots
 c.300 BC Vergina

Burse (detail)
St Stephen's, Meteora

Crucifix;
1670 AD
Meteora

Basilica: Church of Panayia Ahiropitos, Thessaloniki

A good example of the number and quality of un-known churches is demonstrated by the church in the mountain village of Ypati in Boetia, which is not record-ed in general guide books.

A little breakfast at Ypati

Ottoman fountain with Arabic inscription
Nico's Hotel, Ypati

Finally

Any visitor to Greece is not only looking at classical sites, museums, coins, monasteries or buildings, but is visiting a people, country and life. The life of modern Greece is of course the principal memory of my time in Greece. Any street scene is of interest. The small cafes, chatting to neighbours, the tasting of a variety of new foods and local drinks are all as important as the sights and history. It seems right therefore to close with pictures of street scenes and food.

ΟΔΟΣ
ΧΡΥΣΟΣΤΟΜΟΥ
PLAKA with skip and building work from ΙΦΙΝΟΗ (Ifinoi daughter of King
+ Bougainvillea   on 5.2010   Protus

ΞΑΝΤΟΥΙΤΣ = Sandwich
not Santorini wine

"We had a few"!!

Greek beer   Capaccino Freddo   Freshly squeezed oranges   Fried aubergines

How we really got round Greece

Greek tortoise at Old Corinth
about to take the plunge

Sources & Acknowledgements

We have tried to trace the origin and owners of all illustrations used, crediting the owner where possible. We apologise for omissions or inaccuracies. Where requested, the origin of a particular picture has been noted alongside the illustration.

Certain illustrations said to be within the public domain, and therefore available for reproduction, have been provided from photographic libraries.

Coin illustrations are mostly after C.M.Kraay and Max Hunter, *Greek Coins,* (London 1966), with some re-dating by Harold Mattingly. Pheidias' mug is reconstructed fom an illustration in Judith Swaddling, *The Ancient Olympic Games* (British Museum 1980, rep 2011), p 20. Illustrations of pottery beehives are based on *The Archaeology of Beekeeping*, by Eve Crane.

The Authors

Harold Mattingly was Professor of Ancient History at Leeds University, is a past president of the Royal Numismatic Society and a Fellow of the Society of Antiquaries of London. He has always worked in numismatic and epigraphical studies, and his work has often sought and defended unorthodox positions in the fields of numismatics and epigraphy.

Joanna Mattingly is a visual historian, interested in medieval churches, houses and museum artefacts. She has written and advised on many aspects of local and architectural history and, like her father, is an FSA. Her books include a guide to the churches of Cornwall, and a volume on *Cornwall and the Coast* for the *Victoria County History*. Sketching is an integral part of her research and this is the second of her illustrated publications. She and her husband live in Truro.

The city states and countries of the Aegean
Reproduced under free licence United States (CC BY-ND 3.0)